Flowers

Lynn Stone

Rourke
Publishing LLC
Vero Beach, Florida 32964

www.rourkepublishing.com

PHOTO CREDITS: Ally photos © Lynn M. Stone except, pg.4 © Lisa Kyle Young; pg.6 Photographer Olympus; pg.8 Lisa Thornberg; pg.12 Illustration © Renee Brady; pg.16 © Timothy Wood; pg.18 © Monica Armstrong; pg.19 © Willi Schmitz.

Editor: Robert Stengard-Olliges

Cover design by Michelle Moore.

Library of Congress Cataloging-in-Publication Data

Stone, Lynn M.
  Flowers / Lynn Stone.
    p. cm. -- (Plant parts)
  ISBN 978-1-60044-551-4 (Hardcover)
  ISBN 978-1-60044-691-7 (Softcover)
  1. Flowers--Juvenile literature. I. Title.
  QK49.S815 2008
  582.13--dc22
                                    2007015154

Printed in the USA

CG/CG

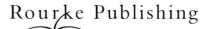

Rourke Publishing

www.rourkepublishing.com – rourke@rourkepublishing.com
Post Office Box 3328. Vero Beach. FL 32964

Table of Contents

People Love Flowers

Flowers are easy to see. They often grow at the top end of a long, green stem. Flowers are often very colorful. Many flowers have a sweet smell.

4

Flowers have many shapes. Some are named for their shape. One is called a lady's slipper. Another is the sunflower.

6

Lady's Slipper

Many flowers have big, colorful **petals**. Look at the flower of a garden rose. It looks like a fistful of petals. But there is far more to a flower than its petals.

8

Petals

New Plants

Flowers are important for reasons other than beauty or smell. Flowers allow plants to make new plants. Flowers are the **reproductive** parts of plants.

11

Different Flower Parts

Look carefully at the center of a flower. There's a lot to see!

These are the male and female parts of the flower. Together, these parts start the growth of new flowers.

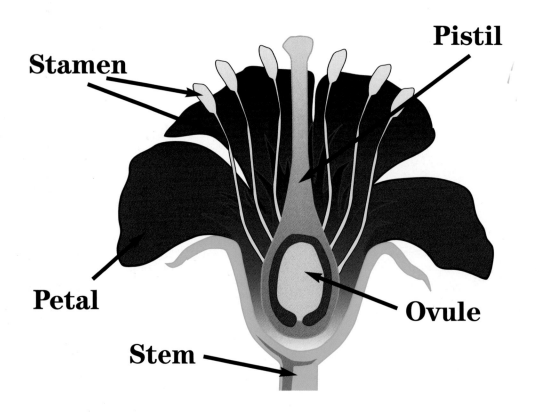

Stamen

Pistil

Petal

Ovule

Stem

12

13

The main female part is the **pistil**. One part of the pistil makes egg cells called **ovules**.

The main male part is the **stamen**. One part of the stamen makes male reproductive cells called **pollen**. Pollen looks like yellow dust.

Pistil

Ovule

Pollen

Stamen

15

How Animals Help

The pollen needs to get to the ovule to make new plants. Animals, called **pollinators**, help move the pollen.

The best known pollinators are bees. But other insects, bats, and birds are also pollinators.

Flowers attract pollinators with their color or smell. Pollen rubs off on a pollinator's body. Then pollen rubs on the ovule of one flower or another.

When pollen reaches an ovule, the ovule makes new seeds. By making seeds, the flower has done its job. New plants will grow from the new seeds.

Ovule

New Seeds

21

Glossary

ovule (oh VULE) — one of a plant's female parts

petal (PET uhl) — flat, colorful parts of a flower blossom

pistil (PISS tuhl) — the main female part of a flower

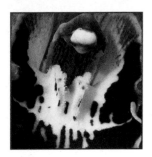

pollen (POL uhn) — yellow grains that include male cells

pollinator (POL uh NA tor) — any animal that moves from flower to flower

reproductive (ree PRO duck tive)— any part of a plant that helps reproduce that plant

stamen (STA men) — a flower's main male part

Index

Further Reading

Bodach, Vijaya. *Flowers*. Pebble Plus, 2007.

Spilsbury, Louise. *Why Do Plants Have Flowers?*. Heinemann, 2006.

Websites to Visit

www.kathimitchell.com/plants.html

www.picadome.fcps.net/lab/currl/plants/default.htm

About the Author

Lynn M. Stone is the author of more than 400 children's books. He is a talented natural history photographer as well. Lynn, a former teacher, travels worldwide to photograph wildlife in its natural habitat.

I1 1   07